SIGNS *of* SURVIVAL

A MEMOIR OF THE HOLOCAUST

RENEE HARTMAN WITH **JOSHUA M. GREENE**

Scholastic Press / New York

Photos ©: 113, 114, 116, 120, 121, 122: Renee G. Hartman; 115: Slovak National Gallery; 117, 118 top: Yad Vashem; 118 bottom: United States Holocaust Memorial Museum, courtesy of National Archives and Records Administration, College Park; 119: Courtesy of Judiska Kvinnoklubben, Stockholm/Association of Jewish Women, Stockholm.

ISBN 978-1-338-75335-6

10 9 8 7 6 5 4   23 24 25

Printed in the U.S.A.   37

First printing November 2021

Book design by Keirsten Geise

To my two children, David and Elizabeth,

and my nephew and nieces,

Ira, Hetty, and Sara

1

The Sound of Boots

RENEE: IN 1943, GERMAN soldiers rounded up the Jews living in my city, Bratislava, and sent them to death camps to be killed. There would be eight to twelve soldiers marching together from house to house, knocking on doors, and yelling, "Get ready to leave! You have one hour!" I remember the stomping of their boots on the cobblestoned streets.

My parents, younger sister, and I lived in a fourth-floor apartment, and when I heard the sound of those boots, I ran to warn my family. Then we rushed into a room at the back of the apartment and hid. When the soldiers knocked on our door, we didn't answer and stayed as quiet as possible.

I was ten years old then, and my sister was eight. The responsibility was on me to warn everyone when the soldiers were coming because my sister and both my parents were deaf.

I was my family's ears.

2

Hidden Stars

HERTA: MY NAME IS Herta Myers. I'm Renee's younger sister. I was born two years after her, in 1935. When I was a little girl, I was the only deaf child in our town. In our family there were several deaf people like me, going back a few generations, including both our parents: our mother, Henrietta, and our father, Julius. We communicated using sign language.

RENEE: We grew up in Bratislava, the capital of what was then called Czechoslovakia. Many years after World War II, Czechoslovakia was split into two independent states, the Czech Republic and Slovakia. Back then, Bratislava was a city of 120,000 people, including 15,000 Jews. In 1939, when the Nazis occupied our city, most of our country was renamed the Slovak Republic, which was then controlled by Germany. Many ethnic Germans lived in and around Bratislava.

Jews living in Bratislava's more elegant neighborhoods were ordered to leave their homes and move into what was called the Old Town, which was a ghetto for the poor. That was where my family began living, in an apartment on the fourth floor of an old four-story brick building. In warm weather, my sister and I grew peas by wrapping them in wet cotton balls. We put the balls into little pots of soil on the windowsill and watched over the next few weeks as pea tendrils sprouted and curled up around the iron railings of the window. From our window, we could also peer down in the evening and see our father returning from his office.

Because the Nazis forbade Jewish children from attending school, I did not start my formal education until after the war, when I was almost twelve years old. By then the only subject I didn't have to catch up on was reading, which my father had started teaching me when I was five years old. I remember how much joy I felt when my parents gave me several books for my fifth birthday. That year my mother was often annoyed with me, because I never answered when she called me. My nose was always buried in my books.

HERTA: Our parents were intelligent people, but because they could not hear, they did not attend a typical college. Instead, they went to the Vienna School for the Deaf. After graduating, my father became a master jeweler, and my mother worked as a dressmaker.

RENEE: Once the Nazis occupied Bratislava in 1939, they regularly entered the homes of Jews and forced them to turn over their jewelry and silverware. Because my father was an expert jeweler, the Slovak firm he worked for ordered him to melt down the stolen silver and use it to make chalices and crosses for local churches. I remember him coming home with designs for these objects and looking so sad.

HERTA: At first my parents wanted me to go to the School for the Deaf like they had done, but after the Nazis took over our city, my parents were scared that I would go to school one day and never come back. So we moved about seventy miles west of Bratislava to Brno, where there was a big Jewish community, and for a while we did feel more comfortable there.

My father tried to homeschool me, but I was lazy and had no interest in most subjects. I'd tell him, "Oh, let's do that subject tomorrow—or maybe the day after." Then I would run outside and walk around Brno with my sister, Renee. Because I was deaf, I had to rely on her to be my playmate, and there were times I complained to my mother that I felt lonely. My mother was always willing to give me her time and attention, so despite the loneliness, I considered myself a happy child.

❧

RENEE: I have one recollection of the German presence at that time, which was when Hitler came through Brno in a car surrounded by Nazi soldiers. All the non-Jews of Brno ran into the streets, cheering and waving Nazi flags, and I remember my father telling me and Herta to stay away from the crowds.

"We are not going to show any support," he said.

I'm sure there was more to it than what my father was saying. He must have known it would be dangerous for us as Jewish children to go outside with so many non-Jews in the streets, cheering Hitler. My father was no doubt afraid that some harm would come to us. As a six-year-old child, I had no idea about politics, although I recall feeling comfortable and uncomfortable at the same time—comfortable because I spoke German like many people around us, but uncomfortable because most of our neighbors hated us because we were Jews.

My parents must have decided things would get worse now that Hitler had visited Brno, and so they announced we would immediately be returning to Bratislava. We had heard what Nazis did to Jews: The Germans arrested them and sent them to "resettlement" camps. In those days, we had not yet heard the name "concentration camps," but whatever they were called, we knew the camps were dangerous for Jews. To avoid the risk of being arrested and sent to a camp, we packed our bags and returned to our apartment in Bratislava.

Back in Bratislava, at first nothing happened to us. German soldiers there just patrolled the streets as usual. Then it got worse. The soldiers began beating up Jews, and local antisemitic Slovaks also abused us and called us "Dirty Jews!" and other nasty things when we passed them in the street.

The abuse got worse once the Nazis forced all Jews to sew a yellow star—the Star of David, a symbol of the Jewish people—on their outer clothing. That was the Nazis' way of singling us out in public. One day Herta and I came home and saw our mother sewing yellow cloth stars on our coats.

"Let's not do this," I signed to her. "If we wear the star, then we can't hide the fact that we are Jews, and it will be worse for us."

"We have no choice," she signed with sadness. "We have to wear the star. It's the law."

Wearing that star was going to make life harder for me and my sister, since we loved to roam freely around the city. We came up with the idea of wearing scarves and draping them around our shoulders so they covered the stars on our coats. That worked for a while, and we continued wandering around Bratislava. Still, we were afraid.

What will happen to us, I wondered, *if they find out we're Jews?*

HERTA: Our mother was always busy at home, making dresses and cleaning the apartment. My father's jewelry store was about a half mile away, and before the Nazis came to Bratislava, I used to visit him there after school. The visits ended once the Nazis arrived and forced us to wear that yellow star. If the Germans caught us without it, there would be trouble. Everyone in Bratislava was registered in the city's official records, and if the Germans wanted to find us, they could easily get our names and addresses.

RENEE: By 1941, our part of the city had become inundated with Jews who had been forced to leave their homes and find a place to live in the segregated Jewish quarter. Our apartment building was completely overcrowded. My parents had been ordered to take in six people in addition to our family. What I did to maintain some sense of freedom was to stay out of our apartment as much as I could. Even though the atmosphere on the streets was by now quite hostile, I preferred being out and about in the city.

Nazis and other antisemites in Bratislava were beating up Jews every day, but strangely never me. I asked a teacher in our neighborhood, "Why do people who hate Jews beat up other Jews but not me?"

"Because you have blond hair," she said.

In those days, the popular idea of a good-looking

German was someone with blond hair and blue eyes. My hair was blond and that seemed to make me a little more acceptable, so I was able to move around town.

The worst thing that I saw when I was walking around Bratislava was the transports. These were truckloads of people, mainly Jews, rounded up by Nazi soldiers and sent to "resettlement" camps. Those transports terrified me. Nazi police stormed into the homes of Jews and yelled, "Get out! Get out quickly! Take only one suitcase!" If anyone tried to take something more, such as a blanket, the Germans grabbed it and threw it on the floor.

During roundups, the police hit people to make them move faster, especially old people, sick people, and children. It was a way of behaving that I had never witnessed, not even in nightmares. Bad dreams were mild compared to what the Germans did. What made it worse was that the Nazis abused

13

the very people to whom the Jewish religion says you should show the greatest kindness, namely the old, the sick, and the young. Everything I saw being done was the opposite of the values I had been taught.

There were perhaps as many as a thousand people at a time in these transports. I personally knew many of the people who were mistreated and sent away, and I could hardly imagine how devastating the experience was for them.

When the Nazis conducted a roundup, they came marching, eight to twelve soldiers at a time. I became good at recognizing the sound of the soldiers' boots on the street outside our window. It was my responsibility to be on guard and warn my deaf sister and our deaf parents of any danger. So I was constantly listening for the sound of those boots. When I heard the soldiers coming or the screams of people being sent away, I'd run to my family and tell them in sign language, "We have to hide."

⚮

HERTA: One day, Renee was walking around town without the yellow star, and the police caught her.

"Where is your star?" they yelled.

She broke away from them and ran home. She burst into our apartment, and my father looked at her coat and asked the same question: "Where is your star?" He was so afraid that something bad was going to happen to us.

Our fears increased every day.

3

The Farm

RENEE: BY 1943, MY parents realized our situation was hopeless and there was no point living in this fearful way. They knew a family with a farm some miles away, in the foothills of the Tatra Mountains, and they asked the husband and wife to please take me and Herta and hide us on their farm. The farm couple agreed, on the condition that my parents pay them a large amount of money each month. Even though the couple insisted on being paid, they were still taking a big risk to their own lives.

❧

HERTA: The couple who owned the farm were also deaf and had met my parents at a meeting of deaf people living in the area. In exchange for the monthly payments, the farmer and his wife let us stay, and they also hid the fact that we were Jewish. We didn't have to go to church, but Renee and I had to pretend we were Christians. For example, when we walked by a priest, we had to cross ourselves.

❧

RENEE: Before my sister and I left to live on that farm, my mother took all the yellow stars off our clothing. Once we arrived there, we pretended to be Christian. I felt terrible crossing myself and worried that we'd be punished in some way for pretending we were Christians, but it worked. We played with the children in the village, and no one suspected we were Jews. Still, it wasn't always fun. Many of the village children didn't have shoes, so they were always trying to take ours. And they poked fun at Herta for being deaf, so after a while we started keeping to ourselves most of the time.

HERTA: The only other person living on the farm was the farmers' son, who was much older than me and Renee. Because we had so few children to play with, we stayed busy watching the grown-ups cut the grass, feed the cows and pigs, make sausages, and do other chores. One day, Renee decided that she would no longer eat the sausages, which were made with pork. We were from a religious Jewish family, and eating pork was forbidden by Jewish dietary laws. Well, I didn't stop eating the sausages, and Renee was ready to disown me. She complained more and more about wanting to go home, and the farmer and his wife were getting fed up with us.

Then my father paid us a surprise visit. Oh, I was so happy to see him. But he warned us that he could stay only one night and that the next morning he would have to go back to Bratislava.

"Why can't you stay longer?" I asked him.

He said, "If a Jew wants to leave town, the Nazis give him an official paper with a time limit of only one day. It's better than nothing."

I agreed.

The next morning, my father came quietly into our room and kissed us on our foreheads.

"Why are you waking me up?" I asked him.

He just kept kissing me and hugging me. I didn't know that this would be the last time I would ever see my father. I have always regretted that I was sleepy and didn't hug him back. I'm sure my father understood I didn't mean to ignore him, but that is one regret I will have for the rest of my life.

4

The Last Jews in Bratislava

RENEE: IN SPRING OF 1944, the farmers' son announced that he and his parents had not heard from our mother and father in a long time. "Your parents have failed to pay for the last five months of your stay," he said, "so now you have to leave." Then he put us in their wagon and drove us back to Bratislava—and just left us there on the street.

I took my sister by the hand, and we walked around looking for a place to stay. One thing I noticed right away was that it seemed the transports had ceased. There were no more roundups, no shouting, and in one sense it was a relief. But in another sense, it was scary, because I realized that we might be the last Jews in Bratislava and that all the others might have been taken away.

There were some non-Jewish people we knew living in Bratislava, and Herta and I went around knocking on their doors, asking if they could tell us where our parents were. They all told us the same thing: They didn't know where our parents were. Later, we found out that our parents had been sent to a concentration camp, but none of our neighbors were willing to tell us. No one explained that our parents had been deported, so we lived with the vain hope that we might find them.

I took Herta to see a mattress maker we knew. He agreed to let us hide at night on the top floor of the building where he had his workshop, even though it was risky for him. During the day, we had to stay out of the building because he had workers there. Some of the workers were antisemitic, and if they knew Jews were hiding there, they'd certainly betray us to the Nazis. For three weeks, Herta and I spent our days walking around Bratislava, going into shops, visiting churches, and wandering all over waiting for night.

After three weeks of living like that, the mattress maker told us his workers had become suspicious because they had found bread crumbs. He was afraid the workers would complain to the Nazi authorities that their boss was hiding Jews, and he told us he couldn't keep us any longer. We had to find some other place to hide. We packed our one little bag, climbed down the stairs, and were again on the streets of Bratislava.

I remember one harrowing episode. Herta and I were walking down a street, and somebody who

had known our parents saw us. He must have recognized me because of my hair, which was short,
blond, and tightly curled.

"Come here!" he shouted. "Don't worry. I'm
going to take care of you."

I was suspicious and careful to watch for any
clues of danger, and I knew immediately I couldn't
trust him. By then I had lost trust in more or less
everybody.

"No," I told him, "we're not going with you," and
I took Herta by the hand, and we started running.

He chased us, so it was a good thing we knew
the streets of Bratislava well. We weaved our way
down streets, around corners, and through little
openings in buildings. Finally, after about twenty
minutes, we managed to lose him.

We were scared of again meeting the man who
had chased us, scared of meeting anyone who knew
we were Jews. We'd been on that farm and away

from the town for about nine months, so I hoped we'd grown tall enough that it would be harder for anyone to recognize us—but what were we to do now? Where could we go?

The thought that my sister and I might be the last Jews in Bratislava was terrifying. I couldn't bear it. I kept thinking, *Have all the other Jews been sent away to be killed? I don't want us to be the last ones alive.*

I held our little suitcase in one hand and Herta with the other hand, and we walked and walked, scrounging for food and looking for a place to stay. I knocked on the doors of anyone we knew who was still there, and they slammed the doors right in our faces—not saying a word, not explaining, just as if we were beggars.

That's when I understood that we were indeed the last Jews in Bratislava.

5

The Train

RENEE: I TOLD HERTA, "We can't live this way. We will die on the street. We might as well just go to the police and turn ourselves in."

So we did. We went to the Slovak police, I gave them my name and our parents' names, and I said we'd like to join our parents wherever they were. The police were amused, and at first they just laughed. Then they realized that I was serious and that presented them with a problem. They didn't know what to do with us.

They told us to sit on a bench while they tried to find out what to do. We spent the whole night sitting on that bench.

They must have found out where our parents were, because the next morning they put us on a truck and we were taken to Hungary, to the town of Sered. This was a pre-camp, a place from which Jews and other victims of the Nazis were deported. At the police station in Sered, there was a nice woman who took us under her care. She said she was going to see what she could do to help us join our parents, and in the meantime, she fed us, gave us blankets and clothing, and we stayed in her home for two weeks.

Because Herta didn't know how to communicate with hearing people, I explained everything to her with sign language. I had to constantly hold her by the hand and didn't dare lose sight of her, because in a crowd we could have easily been separated, and that would have been a disaster.

One morning, the police came to the Sered precamp. They took me and Herta to the train station and put us in a cattle car filled with Jews. In some ways it was a relief, because even though these people were strangers, at least we were among fellow Jews again. Finally, one of the policemen arrived and told us where we were going.

"You are going to join your parents," he said, "in Auschwitz."

That was the first time I heard the word *Auschwitz*. I had no idea it was the largest of Hitler's concentration camps.

6

Betrayed

RENEE: WE WERE ON that train for days, and during the entire trip, our train kept stopping because of bombs falling from British and American aircraft. This was in late summer 1944, the war was slowly coming to an end, and Allied planes were dropping bombs on any trains that might be transporting munitions for the German army. Sometimes the explosions were so loud we thought a bomb had hit our cattle car.

There were hundreds of people crowded into each of those cars. Herta and I sat on our one suitcase the whole time. Once, a bomb exploded so close that our train car skidded off the tracks, and we were stuck there for what seemed like forever. Finally, a German soldier slid open the big wooden door and ordered us to get out.

"Everyone out!" he yelled. "You are going to be rerouted!"

We climbed down from the cattle car, crossed the tracks, and guards pushed us toward another train. Some of the people were so weak they could barely walk. Maybe because my sister and I were young, somehow we still had enough strength to climb up into the other train. Once everyone was again crammed into the new cattle car, guards slammed the door shut and the train departed.

The next day, the train stopped, and guards

opened the big wooden door and threw each of us one slice of bread. The cattle car had straw on the floor and two huge containers, one filled with water to drink and an empty one for use as a toilet. There were so many people crowded into that car that the toilet container quickly filled and spilled over, soaking the straw. The cattle car had no windows, and during the three days we traveled, some people choked from lack of air; others fainted from hunger or exhaustion.

On the third night, the train again stopped. I peered out through narrow spaces between the wooden slats of the car and saw rims of light from windows in nearby houses, so we knew we had arrived at a town, but no one knew exactly where.

Maybe, I told myself, trying to be hopeful, *just maybe, we have been sent back to Bratislava.*

But it was not Bratislava. And it was not

Auschwitz, where we had hoped to rejoin our parents. Soon we would learn that we had been sent to a different concentration camp.

This one was called Bergen-Belsen.

7

Bergen-Belsen

RENEE: THE TRAIN HAD arrived near a town called Celle, about fifteen miles from Bergen-Belsen. All day long, rain pounded loud and relentless on the roof of our cattle car. It was late at night when guards finally opened the door and yelled, "Everybody out! Quickly!"

The guards pushed the prisoners from the train into three rows and marched us down a dirt road into the dark, rainy night. The march was long from the train station to Bergen-Belsen, and for many of the prisoners it was also painful, because we had been traveling with hardly any food or water, and no one was in any shape to walk anywhere.

My sister and I were carrying a small valise with our clothing and a rolled-up blanket that the woman in Sered had given us. The blanket quickly soaked through and grew heavy with rainwater. We staggered on in the rain, and the journey seemed endless. Everyone was so weak and hungry it seemed to take forever.

At one moment, out of exhaustion or confusion, Herta let go of my hand and wandered away. I turned around—and she was gone. She was deaf, so I couldn't call out to her, and she could easily get lost or be killed if a guard thought she was running away. I was in a panic. Finally, I spotted her and rushed over. My hands were full carrying the suitcase and wet blanket, so I couldn't grab her arm.

What could I do to get her attention? I felt I had no choice but to bend down and bite her cheek. Oh, did I regret that. She burst out crying, and I found myself going back and forth between feelings of relief over finding her to anger that she had wandered off.

Herta and I were little children—how did we manage to walk that far, in the rain, hungry and thirsty, carrying a suitcase and a soaking-wet blanket?

Yet we did manage to keep walking, and at last we arrived at Bergen-Belsen.

Prisoners in striped uniforms pushed open the iron gates to the camp, and we stumbled through. Around us, German guards shouted, "Hurry up! Hurry up!" Some of the guards beat prisoners to make them go faster. Others held German shepherds on leashes—big, ferocious dogs that barked loudly at us.

Herta and I were marched to a wooden barrack

with maybe fifty other women and girls. I remember standing inside this barrack and thinking, *I'm so exhausted. I must sleep.* At the same time, I felt a responsibility to notice everything: how things were laid out, where we were supposed to go to the bathroom, what we were supposed to be doing, where the exits were, and where the windows were.

In this barrack, the wooden bunks had three levels made of raw wooden planks with a little straw thrown on them. "No one can take just any bunk!" a guard yelled. "Wait to be given your assigned place!"

I didn't wait but instead rushed with Herta to the bunk nearest to the door. I'm not sure why. Maybe I thought it would be the best bunk if we decided to try to run away. We sat down and stared at our ankle-high shoes covered in mud. Then Herta signed some angry words at me for biting her cheek, and I signed back how terrified I'd been at the thought of losing her.

I had a terrible time falling asleep that first night. We'd had nothing to eat or drink for a long time, and we were starving and scared. I remember thinking as I finally started to fall asleep that life had played a terrible trick on us. We weren't in Auschwitz with our parents like the police in Sered had promised. I vowed to myself that I would never stop looking for our mother and father.

HERTA: That first night it was pouring rain. The guards had taken away our suitcase. My sister and I had only the clothing we were wearing, which was soaking wet, and we had to sleep in those wet clothes.

Renee woke me in the morning. We were shivering from the cold. She signed to me that she heard guards yelling. Renee told me in sign language, "Get up! Get up! We have to get in line!"

Guards rushed all the prisoners from our barrack

outside, where we lined up with the prisoners from the other barracks. We stood there in the cold for a long time while they counted us to be sure no one had tried to escape during the night. The prisoners were so cold and hungry that several people fell to the ground and died right in front of us.

❧

RENEE: The routine of the camp started each day with that morning *appel*, the roll call. That lasted for hours, no matter how bad the weather was. Then there would be "breakfast," if you want to call it that.

❧

HERTA: They gave us one small slice of stale bread and one cup of fake coffee they made by pouring hot water over some fried grains. And that was it. The same for "lunch," and that's all we had to eat every day, again and again.

RENEE: The Germans pushed the prisoners here and there to do hard work around the camp. My sister and I were children, but the guards made us do the same work as the adults. We carried heavy bags of supplies, scrubbed the barrack floor, and emptied buckets from the latrine. I did everything the Germans told us to do. But later I would wander around the camp, asking if anyone knew prisoners who had come from Bratislava and collecting information, finding out everything I could, any information that would help us to survive. I asked the other prisoners about the dangers of the camp, which guards we should avoid, what to say, and what not to say. Some people considered me a pest because I always pushed my way around with my sister holding my hand.

The brutality that we witnessed in Bergen-Belsen was horrible beyond words, like nothing anyone

can imagine. In Bratislava, people had occasion-
ally thrown bricks at us and called us "dirty Jews."
In Bergen-Belsen, we watched people being beaten
and murdered—not for doing something wrong,
but just for being Jews.

My sister and I were in Bergen-Belsen for nearly a
year, and it was a terribly lonely time. We were in
a children's barrack with mostly Polish-speaking
children, and most of the adult prisoners didn't speak
German. They spoke Yiddish, which was a language
spoken by Jews in Central and Eastern Europe at the
time. Eventually, I learned to speak some Yiddish
and began communicating with more people, but
for the first few months, I had few people to talk to.
The soldiers spoke German, and the German language became identical in my mind with the cruelty
of the Nazis. That's when I started learning Polish.

❧

HERTA: Sometimes, when the guards weren't making us do hard work, Renee and I would play with the other kids. We rolled bits of cloth into little balls and played catch. Still, because I was deaf and the other kids didn't know sign language, I always felt left out. If Renee was speaking with other children, I'd sign, "What did they say? What were they saying?" I got angry with her, telling her, "You talk for so long to those people, and yet you only tell me little bits and pieces of what you said."

I really was a pest to Renee because I was so starved for contact with others. Often, she got exhausted from talking to me and I felt so lonely. We were prisoners in Bergen-Belsen for nearly a year, but it seemed to me like a lifetime.

There was barbed wire all around the camp, and people were dying every day. What I saw the Nazis do to people was horrible. And on top of that, I couldn't communicate with anyone.

I tried to stay positive and told Renee, "You'll see. We will get out of here alive, right?"

"No, we won't," she said.

"Yes, we will," I insisted. "We will get out."

But sometimes I also doubted the future and asked myself, *Are we going to live or die here?* I had a devil on one shoulder telling me, "*Yes, you're going to die,*" and I had an angel on the other shoulder telling me, "*No, you're going to live.*"

"Think positively," I told Renee. "Think positive thoughts." I was saying that to myself as well.

Sometimes we argued about it. Those moments were difficult because we were sisters, we loved each other, and we wanted to support each other and stay as positive as possible.

But how can anyone stay positive in a concentration camp?

8

Monster Doctors

RENEE: WHEN JEWS AND other prisoners arrived at Bergen-Belsen, I would go to the barbed-wire fence and search the crowd, looking for our parents. One of the soldiers got irritated with me because every time new prisoners arrived, I asked him in German, "Can I please call out my mother's name?" My mother was deaf, but I thought if she was among the new prisoners, maybe someone would tell her they heard me calling her name.

By the fifth or sixth time I did that, the soldier lost his temper. He picked me up and flung me down against a stone and knocked me unconscious. The blow made me temporarily deaf, which worried me tremendously because I had to be my sister's ears, and I was afraid that the soldier had permanently damaged my hearing. After about five or six days, my hearing came back, but since that time I've always had hearing problems. Even today I wear a hearing aid.

One day, I noticed that my sister was being watched by one of the Nazi officers, whose name was Josef Kramer. Kramer was the *kommandant*, or head, of Bergen-Belsen. He showed up several times at the children's barrack, walked over to my sister, pinched her cheeks, gently pulled her ears, and pretended to be friendly with her. It was clear to me that he and the so-called doctors on his staff were doing something to the children, but I didn't know what it was. These men were not doctors in any normal sense but monsters who used prisoners for their terrible experiments.

❧

HERTA: One of these "doctors" came into the children's barrack and announced that my sister and I had to be examined. They took us to the prisoner hospital and asked us all sorts of questions. When Renee told them that I was deaf, the doctors had a discussion, and I was sure they wanted to kill me. Renee thought the same thing, and she lost her mind and ran over to them and bit one of the doctors— just bit him! She could have been killed for doing that. But she loved me so much that she would have preferred to die than break her promise to take care of me.

❧

RENEE: The doctor could easily have killed me, but he wanted me to encourage my sister to go with him, so he tried to reason with me. He said, "If you let us keep Herta in the hospital for a few days, we'll give you oranges and chocolates." Herta didn't need to go to any hospital. She was perfectly well.

I was sassy and defiant. "No," I told him, "you are not going to put her in the hospital! And if you try to take her, I'm going to kick you! I'm serious! I mean it!"

The doctor laughed at me and walked away.

When Herta and I were brought back to our barrack, one of the prisoners told me that the Nazi doctors wanted to use my sister for their "scientific research." At the time, I had no idea what that meant, but later I realized they were interested in experimenting on a child who was deaf. One thing the adult prisoners always told us was, "Never agree to go to the prisoner hospital, even if you are very ill. The Nazi doctors are not to be trusted."

⌒∽

HERTA: There were a lot of kids in the children's barrack. Some had parents who were being held in some other part of Bergen-Belsen. Some children had no one because their parents had been killed by the Nazis.

When the Germans built Bergen-Belsen, they made separate sections, one for the men and another for the women. Our camp was just for women and children. Renee and I had no idea what was going on in other parts of the camp. We were just looking to survive one more day. I felt like the Germans had put us in a cage. Looking back today, I'm shocked that we survived. All I can say is, "Thank you, God, for giving me the strength to go on," because each day all I could think was, *Am I going to die today?* That was the only question I had.

One day, the doctors again decided to examine me. This time they checked my scalp and found I had lice in my hair. Lice carried typhus and other deadly diseases, so the doctors wanted to shave off all my hair. Renee overheard them, but she didn't want to scare me, so she chose not to tell me what they were going to do.

The next afternoon, a doctor came into our barrack and motioned with his hand for me to come over to him, but I shook my head no. I refused. Another man came in and spoke with him, then together they came toward me. I was so afraid. What was going on? I saw one man had a big pair of scissors. Was he going to murder me? They grabbed me, and one man held me while the other one cut off all my hair. I screamed, but they didn't stop until I was completely bald.

Afterward, I understood that they didn't want me infecting the other prisoners, but that may have been pointless because there were lice everywhere. When we went to bed at night, we saw thousands of lice climbing all over the walls.

After they shaved my head, Renee told me in sign language, "I couldn't tell you because I know you have a temper and would just yell at me." I hated my sister for not preparing me, for not telling me what they were going to do or why. I felt like I was the only child on earth who looked that way. I found a cloth cap and wore it every day, and every morning I would check to see if my hair was growing back. Finally, after many weeks it did grow back, and I got rid of the cap.

Getting my hair cut off wasn't so bad compared to the punishment and starvation that other prisoners were made to suffer. There were much worse things in Bergen-Belsen. We watched people get shot. We saw people die from sickness and hunger.

RENEE: Right across from the children's barrack was a building filled with dead bodies, not just inside but overflowing outside as well. I lived and walked beside dead people. After a while, we had to say to ourselves, *I'm not going to look at who this is. I'm not going to recognize a person lying here.*

I had to close my eyes to a number of things. Otherwise I would not have survived.

During the entire time we were in Bergen-Belsen, we never saw a calendar. We had no idea what day it was, what month it was, or what year it was. We only knew what season it was because it snowed in winter and grew unbearably hot in summer.

HERTA: One day, my sister came down with typhoid fever. She grew weaker and weaker until I was sure she was going to die. She was suffering so much that she didn't want to live anymore. I watched over her and told her to be strong, but she kept saying she had nothing to live for.

"Please! Please, Renee. Stay with me," I begged her. This was in the beginning of April 1945.

Things changed completely just a few days later.

9

April 1945—FREEDOM

HERTA: ONE AFTERNOON, AN army truck drove into Bergen-Belsen. It was not like any truck we'd seen before. The soldiers wore uniforms different from the Nazis', and one of the prisoners told us these soldiers were from England. The war was over.

As soon as they arrived, the German guards changed out of their uniforms, put on prisoners' clothes to hide their identities, and ran away into the surrounding forest. When the prisoners saw that the Nazis were running away and that British soldiers had taken over the camp, they started throwing rocks at the fleeing Germans. I was confused by this. I didn't want to get into trouble and asked my sister, "What's going on? Why are prisoners throwing rocks?"

Renee was weak from typhus, but she looked at me with a big smile and signed, *"We're free!"*

"Free?" I asked her. I was in shock. "I mean, that's impossible, we can't be free . . ."

Even though for so long I'd tried to be the brave one, actually I'd always been afraid that we would be killed. But now—we were free!

RENEE: One of the saddest things in my life has been that I have no recollection of our liberation because I was so ill with typhus. I have no memory of what happened when the British soldiers liberated Bergen-Belsen. I don't remember any of the things people told me afterward about the trucks coming in or the shouts of joy.

One of the British soldiers was a doctor—a *real* doctor—and he carried me into a barrack they had converted into a hospital. He told me later that when they found me I had been near death. If I'd had to wait even two days more for the British to arrive, I would not have survived.

On the other hand, I do have a vivid memory of another joyful day. Sometime after liberation, when my strength had returned, a group of us children were allowed outside the camp. We hiked through a field of lupine flowers of many different colors, growing as far as the eye could see. The lupines stood as tall as me, and each one was topped with a foot-high tower of tiny flowers. It was a glorious sight, and I felt so grateful that despite the misery and deaths of the Holocaust, nature had remained alive and flowers still grew.

~~∂~~

HERTA: Sometime after Renee started to get some strength back, she spoke with a British officer. Then she came to me and signed, "The British are moving us to another place."

"Where?" I asked her. "What other place are you talking about?"

"They're moving us to Sweden," she said. "They have a place there for young people like us who have been separated from their parents."

"No!" I told her in sign language. "I want to go home. I want to go back home to Mommy and Daddy."

"We can't," she signed back.

"Why not?" I asked her.

"Because," she said, "they're still trying to find Mommy and Daddy. We don't know if they're alive or not. A British officer promised me that if they find our parents, we can all go back together to Bratislava."

So we were sent by ship from Germany to Sweden.

10

Summer 1945—SWEDEN

HERTA: WHEN WE ARRIVED in Sweden, at first we stayed at a place provided by the Red Cross for young refugees. Children stayed there until the Red Cross officers found them a decent home.

RENEE: As soon as we arrived, I was put in the care of a Swedish doctor who decided to fatten me up, because at age eleven I weighed no more than a three-year-old child. I had a potbelly, which can happen when you are severely undernourished. It took many weeks, but slowly I regained my health.

Curiously and thankfully, my sister had survived Bergen-Belsen without too much illness. But the horrors she had seen there turned her into a quiet, sullen child who seemed totally cut off from the world. The Swedish women who took care of us were kind, but the only person Herta could talk to was me, and during the months that I was sick, she'd gone completely mute.

HERTA: One day, during late springtime or early summer of 1946, the lady in charge of us at the Red Cross shelter called my sister into her office. When Renee came out, she looked angry and just kept walking. I got up, ran after her, and found her crying against a wall.

"What's wrong?" I asked, but she wouldn't answer me. She just kept crying.

"Is it our parents?" I asked.

"Yes." She nodded.

"Are they dead?" I signed.

Renee nodded again.

I was shocked. I didn't know what to feel or what to say. All I knew in that moment was that this was my sister, and I needed to comfort her. In the back of my mind, I also knew we would never go back to Bratislava. There was nothing and no one for us there anymore.

So there we were in Sweden, and I thought, *This is it. We'll be living here forever.*

The Red Cross officials found a family willing to let us live with them. They had a home near Malmö, a coastal town in southern Sweden. We went there by train, and again I was the only deaf child in the area. I could lip-read, but I had such a hard time understanding what anyone was saying. When we had to write anything in school, I'd cheat and look at the paper of the girl sitting beside me.

The teacher noticed that I wasn't able to do the schoolwork on my own, so she spoke with Renee.

"You need to help your sister," she said.

Renee started attending classes with me, and she tried her best to help me by showing me how to write out the assignments. Sometimes it worked, and I was able to follow the lesson, but Renee had to be there every day, and it was exhausting for her. And when she grew tired, I got angry. I was young and in grief over finding out our parents were dead, and sometimes I took it out on my sister. She understood how frustrated I was.

"Something else has to be done," she told my teacher. "My sister will never be happy being the only deaf child in the whole school."

The school officials started looking for a school for the deaf, and they found a place in Stockholm, the capital of Sweden.

"Do you want to go to Stockholm, to a school for the deaf?" Renee asked me.

"Oh, yes, yes!" I said. I got so excited. My first school! But then it hit me. This would also be our first separation. All our lives, Renee and I had never been apart.

Within a few days, the teacher brought me to the station, and I traveled by train to Stockholm.

It was thrilling to attend a school where all the kids were deaf like me. At first, learning to sign in Swedish was difficult, but I picked it up quickly—and the other children and I were able to communicate!

At night, though, when I lay in my bed in the dark, I truly missed my sister. She was about 370 miles away, and I was only able to see her once a year when my school closed for summer vacation. But those vacations were wonderful. The Red Cross paid for my ticket, I took the train back to Malmö, and Renee and I spent summers together. That made me so happy.

RENEE: Herta and I ended up staying in Sweden for three years. Meanwhile, we had relatives in Brooklyn, New York, who were searching for us. There was an American radio station that broadcast the names of people who had survived the war, and our relatives listened to that station all the time. One day they heard my name on the radio, and they immediately got in touch with the Red Cross.

HERTA: One of our American cousins came to Sweden and told the Red Cross that she was our relative and wanted to bring us back with her to the United States. They gave her permission, and so in 1948, my sister and I left Sweden. By then I was thirteen years old. We flew on a plane—it was our first airplane ride. The plane made several stops to refuel, so it took us twenty-four hours to fly to New York. It was so exciting.

11

1948—NEW YORK

RENEE: COMING TO THE United States in 1948 was a shock. We arrived in August, on one of the hottest days in the history of the United States. We had come from Sweden, where the weather was cool, and I emerged from the plane in New York City and remember thinking, *This is just too hot to bear.*

I turned to the airline official and said, "I'm going back."

But I didn't go back. I looked around the airport

at all the people waiting there. It may be hard to understand my reaction today, but in Bratislava, where Herta and I grew up, there were few people of color. And afterward, in Sweden, nobody had explained to us about the diverse population of the United States. That day was my first time seeing African Americans, and I realized that there were many kinds of people in America.

At the bottom of the exit ramp there were people waving at us and crying out, "Renee! Herta! Renee! Herta!" These were our American relatives—cousins, aunts, and uncles—but we'd never met any of them before. They were from Europe but had left long before my sister and I were born.

Hearing them call our names, I knew we were in the right place, but it was so strange not only being in such a different culture but also with relatives we didn't know. I remember my father telling me once when I was little that I had an aunt who lived in Palestine (in what is today Israel), but suddenly here she was in New York, along with so many other family members we'd never met.

Our family drove us out of the airport, and soon we arrived in Brooklyn. From the window of the car, I saw food stands everywhere, carts and wagons piled high with fruits and vegetables. I was stunned. I couldn't believe it. So much food was a shocking contrast with the scarcity we'd known in Europe. I'd never seen so much food before.

In Sweden, like so many other places in Europe after the war, there were still shortages, and food was rationed. To see so much food, just out there, available on the streets—ice cream, hot dogs, pretzels—all this food, all this abundance!

As I was having these thoughts, I realized that it was a strange world. Not only did we have to get used to war, which was unbearable—but now we had to get used to peace, which was unbelievable.

∼⁀◇⁀∽

HERTA: One day when I was thirteen, I was walking with our cousins on Coney Island beach in Brooklyn, and we noticed some people using sign language. My cousins went up to them and asked, "Do you know where there is a school for the deaf where our cousin could go?"

"Oh, yes," they said. "There are a few schools for the deaf nearby."

My cousins took the names of the schools, and that's how eventually I ended up attending the Lexington School for the Deaf in New York City. There I learned to sign in English. I attended classes there for only a couple of years, and then my relatives decided I should learn a useful trade to earn a living. So, unfortunately, I obtained only a few years of education as a young person, but somehow I managed well.

Soon after leaving school, I met the young man who would become my husband. His name was Herbert Rothenberg. Eventually, we got married and had three beautiful children. All three were also born deaf.

When our children were a bit older, I decided the time had come for me to go to work. I found a job, but two years later my husband died suddenly. So I left my job to look after our three children.

A few years after that, I met my second husband. His name was Richard Myers. We were married only four months when sadly he, too, died, and I was again alone to raise my three children. I found a job in a bank, where I worked for seventeen years.

When the bank was taken over by a bigger bank, I was given a chance to retire. I retired and moved to Las Vegas, Nevada, where I live now.

RENEE: When I was in my teens, I moved to New Haven, Connecticut, where I studied library science at Southern Connecticut State University and became a librarian. In 1956, I married Geoffrey Hartman. Geoffrey was born in Frankfurt and had left Nazi Germany in 1939 on a *Kindertransport*, a train to evacuate children from Nazi-occupied territory to safety in other countries. This was a rescue effort that brought thousands of refugee Jewish children to Great Britain between 1938 and 1940. After coming to America, Geoffrey taught for forty years in the Yale University English department and became Sterling Professor of English and Comparative Literature. He and I had two children. Our daughter is named Liz, and our son is named David. Geoffrey died in 2016.

One of the achievements of which I am most

proud was working with Geoffrey to help create the Fortunoff Video Archive for Holocaust Testimonies at Yale. At the Archive, survivors record their memories of the Holocaust on video. Scholars then discuss how video testimonies differ from printed testimonies and how videos are useful in examining history and the workings of memory. The book you are holding is based in large part on video testimony I recorded for the Fortunoff Video Archive in 1979.

What is left for me after surviving the Holocaust is an impression that there are really two of me, two selves living simultaneously. One is the person who lived before the Holocaust, and the other is the person who lived afterward—the pre-wartime me and the post-wartime me. They are both me; they are connected, but they can't be reconciled—they will never become just one person. They will always be different. It took me a while to realize that not only are these two selves never going to become one person but that I don't want them to. I want them to remain separate.

I don't want the earlier me, the one who experienced the Holocaust, to ever be lost or forgotten.

12

Return to Bratislava

HERTA: THE DAY I stopped working at the bank, Renee said, "Now that you've retired, I can take you with me back to Bratislava."

"Go back to Bratislava? Never!" I told her. "I don't want to go back there. I don't think I can face the pain of remembering what we went through."

"Please say yes," Renee said.

I didn't understand why she was so insistent, but I thought, *Renee went out of her way for me so many times in those sad days. Here's a chance for me to go out of my way for her.* So at last I agreed.

I met Renee at New York's John F. Kennedy airport. We boarded the airplane and sat next to each other.

"You know what?" I signed to her. "The last time we sat on a plane together was when we came to the United States. Now we're sitting beside each other going back to Bratislava. This is our first time back home; I'm fifty-seven years old—and I don't understand. Why did you want me to come with you on this trip?"

My sister smiled at me and signed, "How could I go back without you? Nothing is the same without you."

Our first stop was Vienna, Austria, where my son joined us, and the following day the three of us took an overnight train to Bratislava. We arrived in the morning—and I was stunned. Everything seemed tiny.

"What happened to this station?" I asked Renee. "It's so much smaller than when we were children."

She laughed. "No," she signed back, "it's the same. You just got bigger."

I looked around and said, "This was always a beautiful town." I pointed to a tower in the distance and said, "On top of that tower, there used to be a stone eagle."

My son walked ahead and looked up, then pointed to something and signed to us, "You're right, Mother. The eagle is still there."

From the station, we walked to the street where our apartment used to be. When we arrived, I looked around and my heart broke. All I could do was cry, remembering the pain, the murders, the horrors we had known as children.

We ended our visit, and just before we left Bratislava, Renee turned to me and said, "The real reason I wanted you to come with me was so we could say farewell to our sad youth. The Nazis sent us to Bergen-Belsen before we could have a real childhood. That was a tragedy beyond our control, and as children all we knew was war and suffering. I wanted us to come back here so that we could say goodbye and have some peace at last."

～

HERTA: The peace didn't come right away. Ever since our relocation to Sweden and then after beginning our new lives in America, I'd been having nightmares. As an adult, my nightmares were about people showing up at my home and taking away my children. The nightmares never went away, and I accepted that there would be things I'd have to live with for the rest of my life.

But our visit to Bratislava had another effect on me. From the time we arrived in Sweden after the war until that day when we returned to Bratislava, one of my recurring dreams was about that eagle-shaped landmark atop the tower in our town. The tower had a name: the Michael's Tower, and our apartment building was just one block away. In the dream, our apartment was dark and empty.

After we returned to the United States, I had just one more dream of that tower, and in the dream I saw our apartment—but this time the edges of the windows were glowing with some kind of warm light coming from inside. Ever since then, I have never dreamed of that tower again.

I think that dream meant that I was at peace now. I'd seen my original home one more time and finally said goodbye.

13

Return to Bergen-Belsen

RENEE: BY 2009, THE German government had
rebuilt the grounds of the former concentration
camp Bergen-Belsen into a memorial site. Buses of
schoolchildren lined the parking area, and crowds
of visitors streamed through the newly completed
museum. Just past the museum building, on the
grounds of the former camp, were large rectangular
earthen mounds. Each mound featured a brass sign
indicating that under the mound were thousands of

bodies. The exact number of bodies was unknown, because at the time of liberation, the British had to bury the dead quickly to avoid the spread of disease.

There were also symbolic gravestones here and there around the grounds, placed after the war by family members to commemorate relatives who perished in the camp. Among them was a stone bearing the names of Anne Frank and her sister, Margot, commissioned by their father. Anne Frank was a Jewish girl who grew up in Amsterdam and went into hiding during the war but was eventually captured and taken to Auschwitz and then Bergen-Belsen. Both Anne and her sister died in Bergen-Belsen from typhus. Herta and I never met Anne Frank, but she became famous all over the world for her diary, which her father had published after the war, in 1947.

At another place on the grounds was a tall obelisk built by the Russian government to honor the

Russian soldiers who were among the first to be murdered in Bergen-Belsen.

In January 2009, my husband, Geoffrey, was invited to Bergen-Belsen for a conference about the memorial site's newly completed documentation center. For years I had been reluctant to return to the place where my sister and I had experienced such horrors, but I did not want my eighty-year-old husband to travel alone in winter.

I thought I would have a difficult time returning to Bergen-Belsen. I did not want to remember those terrible days. But by January 2009, I was in my seventies, and I found myself tougher than I had been as a girl—although not completely. It's impossible to be indifferent to sorrow and pain. Maybe my most pronounced emotion as I revisited Bergen-Belsen was sadness over realizing that the world's worst catastrophes are often human-made and that the image of our world today as civilized is a myth. We just became more sophisticated at how we go about killing people.

The interior of the two-story Bergen-Belsen museum was remarkably simple. The long lower floor featured video screens every five feet or so. Each screen showed a survivor of the camp recounting his or her memories. The first floor also had glass cases displaying photos, metal cups and plates, eyeglasses, diaries, and other artifacts from the camp. At the end of the ground floor was a large window looking out on the campgrounds. The effect was quite eerie, knowing that the displays inside the museum were evidence of what had happened outside.

As I examined photos of children—photos taken before liberation, when the concentration camp was still operating—I recognized some of them from the children's barrack where Herta and I were imprisoned. I came upon photos of Otto Klein and Lusia Wolkowicz, who had been in the same children's barrack and then later with us in Sweden. How they looked in the photos was exactly how I remembered them.

Even so, there were gaps in the exhibits. Too many of the photos gave no indication of the children's names. Their identities had disappeared beneath the burial mounds.

The most difficult part of returning to Bergen-Belsen had nothing to do with shortcomings in the museum exhibits, which overall were powerful and well done. Rather, most difficult for me was my own inability to understand what had happened and why. There was no religious or philosophical explanation that made sense. Nor could any museum, however well designed, explain how some people could turn so brutal toward their fellow human beings. No memorial will ever repair such deep losses.

Just before leaving to return to America, Geoffrey and I toured the grounds one last time. The concentration camp barracks were gone—the British military had burned them to the ground in 1945 to contain the spread of disease—and the grounds now were nicely landscaped. Nothing hinted any longer at what had happened. We knew that beneath our feet were the remains of tens of thousands of Nazi victims. Nearly 50,000 had been murdered in Bergen-Belsen.

Did the schoolchildren touring this nicely landscaped memorial site understand what that meant? The Holocaust was rarely mentioned in school curricula at the time, and if it was, teachers had little time to explain this complex period of history. What can young people truly understand of that dark time?

Even I, who lived through it, looked back on our tour of the site and thought, as we left for the airport, *Yes, that is how it was.* And almost immediately, the thought followed, *I can't believe that it really happened.*

The Holocaust was a tragedy so vast, so immense, that even those who experienced it have a hard time accepting what their eyes have seen.

14

A Toilet-Paper Diary

RENEE: WHEN MY SISTER and I had first arrived in the United States from Sweden, I was fifteen years old and determined to tell everybody about our horrible experiences in Bergen-Belsen. I spoke about it on every possible occasion, but my relatives couldn't bear to listen. They told me I had to replace my experiences from the past with the experiences of the Jewish people today. It was too hard for them to hear what I had to say.

Because my family was unwilling to listen to such memories, I searched for other people to tell them to. But no one wanted to listen to what I had to say. So I decided to write. Around age sixteen, a little over a year after arriving in the United States, I wrote a story based on my experiences in Bergen-Belsen. It was my first attempt at writing in English other than high school homework.

My relatives found the story interesting enough to send it to *Ladies' Home Journal* and other women's magazines. All the editors returned the story to me with notes saying that the story was "not appropriate for their magazine." I guess I agreed with them, because their magazines were mostly about beauty tips, cooking, ways to be good wives, and how to raise children. It would take many more years before magazines would be ready to publish stories about the darker side of human experience.

One central episode in my life occurred inside

Bergen-Belsen, and it was the event that led me to become a writer. In the camp I found a roll of toilet paper. I swapped something I possessed in exchange for a pencil and secretly started writing on the toilet paper. I wrote about what was happening to me, about my longings, my fears, things I saw, and conversations I overheard.

In one of the barrack searches while we prisoners were outside for roll call, a German guard found this roll of toilet paper. When I came back inside from the roll call, I saw the guard sitting on the lower bunk, holding my toilet-paper diary, rolling it out, reading it to another guard, and laughing. He found it amusing. I rushed over and tried to snatch it back, but he pulled it away.

"No," he said. "This is too good for you."

I had heard the guards' conversation and remember one of them saying to the other, "She has a wonderful sense of humor."

I didn't remember writing anything funny in it.

The guard took my toilet-paper diary, and they left. I remember saying to myself, *They may have taken my diary, but they can't stop me from writing.* That was when I vowed that I would spend the rest of my life writing.

Ever since, I have been writing poems and stories about the Holocaust. I also write about things in my imagination, and I've discovered that imaginary experiences are as important as historic experiences.

It doesn't matter to me if anyone will read what I write. I have the desire to write, and I write. That's what matters.

Lost

For Herta

Do you remember

how the peach ran

down tongues,

how honeyed

the ordinary?

How winged

mother's kisses

how firm

the father presence

rock hope

that made

night bearable?

Do you remember

skin wearing marks

the air in mouths

where bread was?

Do you remember

days living bravely?

Do you remember

a voice breathing

hold on, hold on

as sleep

grasped the cup

falling upward?

Do you remember

distrusting

sweets of the earth

before snow

and slime

buried your hand's

trace?

Do you remember

the scream,

I forgive you

God

I forgive you?

Can you remember?

Epilogue

By Joshua M. Greene

THE HOLOCAUST WAS THE systematic, state-sponsored murder of six million Jewish men, women, and children by Germany's Nazi party during World War II. The Nazi Party targeted other minorities for persecution and death, but Jews alone were singled out for total destruction.

When Adolf Hitler, head of the Nazi Party, was appointed chancellor of Germany in 1933, he began building his political and military power and eliminating all opposition. His assault against the Jews was uniquely cruel. It began with a boycott of Jewish businesses, followed by hundreds of other decrees that one by one stripped Jews of their legal and civil rights. For instance, Jews could no longer work for the German government. Jews had to turn in their bicycles, their radios, and their jewelry. Jewish children could no longer attend public schools.

Soon after, Nazis removed all books written by Jews from libraries and bookstores. The books were burned in public bonfires, and within a few years, the burning of Jewish books turned into the burning of Jewish people. Between 1933 and 1945, Nazi Germany established approximately 42,000 camps of various types to imprison Jews and other "enemies" from across Europe: concentration camps, labor camps, prisoner of war camps, transit camps, and killing centers called extermination camps or death camps. More than six million Jews and millions of other so-called enemies were murdered in these camps. Their bodies were then burned in crematorium ovens and open pits. The word *Holocaust* itself is derived from Greek, meaning "burnt sacrifice."

By late 1944, conditions inside the camps were rapidly deteriorating. Bergen-Belsen, where Renee and Herta were imprisoned, was originally planned as a camp for "special" Jews who might be exchanged for German prisoners being held abroad. By the second half of 1944, however, Bergen-Belsen had become the destination for thousands of emaciated inmates from other camps. Barracks originally built for one hundred prisoners now housed three hundred or more, with hardly any food left for any of them.

Conditions became even worse after December 1944, when new transports swelled the camp population. Between February 1945 and the liberation of the camp two months later, 35,000 prisoners died.

Bergen-Belsen was originally designed to accommodate 20,000 prisoners, but when British soldiers liberated the camp on April 15, they discovered more than 60,000 prisoners inside, most of them half-starved and seriously ill, and another 13,000 corpses lying around the camp waiting to be buried. The inadequate food rations had shrunk even further, and a typhus epidemic was raging through the camp. Another 14,000 died in the weeks after liberation. Renee was one of thousands of prisoners who contracted typhus and barely survived.

Some of the men, women, and children who survived the Holocaust chose to describe what they endured. Renee and her sister are two of more than four thousand witnesses to the Holocaust who were interviewed for the Fortunoff Video Archive for Holocaust Testimonies at Yale University, the oldest Holocaust survivor video archive in the world. For more than forty years, scholars at the Fortunoff

Video Archive have taped witness testimonies, cataloged these videotapes by subject matter, and produced educational programs that are made available to educators.

The first time I met Renee Hartman was at a restaurant in New Haven, Connecticut, where she had agreed to join me for lunch. Some years before, scholars at the Fortunoff Video Archive had interviewed Renee. I'd watched that interview so many times that meeting her in person felt like a reunion. I began by asking her to tell me more details about her childhood.

"I used to go to the movies by myself," she said. "By the time I was nine, the Nazis had occupied Bratislava and forbidden Jews to enter movie houses. Only non-Jews were allowed in, but my father and I had a trick. When we arrived at the movie house, I took off my coat with the yellow star sewn on and gave the coat to my father. He waited outside while I pretended to be a non-Jew and went in to see the movie. I had curly blond hair and didn't look very Jewish, so the trick worked. My hair was so blond and curly that people said I looked like Shirley Temple."

In those days, Shirley Temple was the most famous of all Hollywood movie stars. She could sing, dance, and act, and by age six had already starred in sixteen movies. She was the idol of children around the world, including Renee and most of the other nine-year-old girls in Bratislava. For Renee's birthday that year, her parents bought her a tiny photo of Shirley Temple.

"I hid the photo in a handkerchief," Renee told me over lunch, "and I kept it with me the whole time my sister and I were in the concentration camp Bergen-Belsen."

In the cheery New Haven restaurant, with food piled before us, it was difficult to imagine what

Renee looked like back then, when British soldiers liberated Bergen-Belsen and she was so ill and skinny that, at age eleven, she weighed less than a three-year-old.

After liberation, Red Cross doctors sent Renee and Herta to Sweden to regain their health. Three years later the sisters traveled by plane from Sweden to America, where they lived with aunts and uncles in Brooklyn. Renee arrived with her Shirley Temple photo, along with souvenirs of Sweden: a collection of colorful bird feathers, flat rocks for skimming, and a collection of Hebrew-language magazines called *Jewish Stars of the World*. The magazines featured photos of movie starlet Hedy Lamarr, actress Lauren Bacall, renowned actors Kirk Douglas and Burgess Meredith, and other popular celebrities.

"As a little girl, I was starstruck," Renee admitted, "but one of the most satisfying moments for me was in 1989, when President George H. W.

Bush appointed Shirley Temple to be the United States ambassador to Czechoslovakia. She served as ambassador for three years and was the first and only woman to hold that position. I never met her, but I was delighted that the little child who sang and danced and showed her dimples turned into such a remarkable woman."

Hearing Renee talk about her childhood helped me understand the importance of witness testimony. In high school, I'd learned about the Holocaust the way most students did: through history books and documentaries that explored antisemitism or described Adolf Hitler's appeal for Germans living in poverty after their nation's defeat in World War I. And like many other high school students, I thought that was as much as I needed to know about that sad time.

When I heard Renee describe her personal experiences—even something as simple as how she sneaked in to see a Shirley Temple movie—it showed me not only how little I understood of survivors' humanness but also how powerful their experiences were when expressed in their own words.

When you watch video testimony, all you see is a person sitting in one place, talking to a video camera. In film school, the first thing students learn is to never show people talking to the camera for too long. "Talking heads won't hold viewers' attention," film students are told. Yet video testimony—either on a screen or reprinted on the pages of a book such as this one—is nothing but "talking heads," and it is still riveting.

In this book, you have read Renee's and Herta's video testimonies, transcribed and edited together. In some places, a few phrases were added for the sake of clarity or to fill in details about where or why an action was taking place. Otherwise, what you have is Renee's story told in her own words, along with additional information provided by her sister, Herta.

The Nazis took away their victims' names, their homes, their families, their hair and clothing, and finally their lives in an attempt not only to murder all Jews but also to wipe their very memory out of human history. This book is an attempt to restore to Renee and Herta the voices, identities, and memories that the Nazis sought to destroy.

Photographs

Surviving members of Renee and Herta's family found photos of them after the war, and sent the photos to Renee and Herta in New York. You can see some of those photographs here, along with other photos from the time period they lived in.

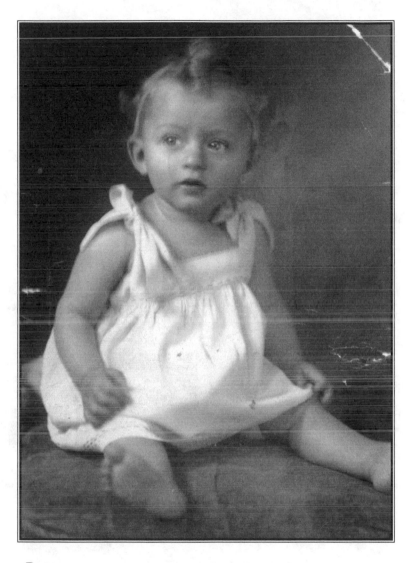

Renee was born in 1933 in Bratislava, which today is the capital of Slovakia.

Renee's family, from left to right: Herta, Henrietta (mother), Renee, and Julius (father).

Bratislava in the 1930s.

Herta, age nine, on left. Renee, age ten and a half, on right.

Children in the Jewish quarter of Bratislava.

Deportation of Jews from Bratislava.

Female prisoners in Bergen-Belsen.

Refugees arriving in Malmö, Sweden, after the war.

Renee at age fifteen, soon after arriving in America.

Renee, newly married and adjusting to life in
America after the war.

This family photo from 1991 shows Renee (on the far right) and
her husband, Professor Geoffrey Hartman, with their
son, David; daughter, Liz; and Liz's baby son, Shel.

About the Authors

Renee Hartman was born in Bratislava, which was then part of Czechoslovakia, and is now the capital of Slovakia. She and her sister were arrested by the Nazis and imprisoned in Bergen-Belsen, where they endured horrifying conditions, and where Renee nearly succumbed to typhus. After being liberated, Renee and her sister immigrated to the United States. Ever since, Renee has been writing about her experiences in the Holocaust. She lives in Connecticut.

Joshua M. Greene produces books and films about the Holocaust. His documentaries have been broadcast in twenty countries and his books translated into eight languages. He has taught Holocaust history for Fordham and Hofstra Universities. He lives in Old Westbury, New York.

Look for these other powerful true
stories of the Holocaust.

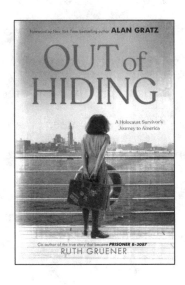

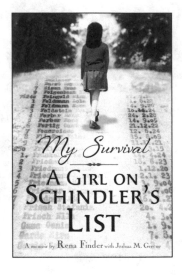